Virtual Reality in Social Work
Changing Lives through Immersive Technologies

Table of Contents

1. Introduction 1

2. The Dawn of Virtual Reality in Social Work 2

    2.1. The Advent of VR and its Integration in Social Work 2

    2.2. Evolving Applications of VR in Social Work 2

    2.3. Extant Research on VR in Social Work 3

    2.4. Challenges and Limitations 4

    2.5. The Future of VR in Social Work 4

3. Decoding Virtual Reality: Context and Mechanics 5

    3.1. Understanding the Technology Behind VR 5

    3.2. The Role of Interactivity 6

    3.3. The State of VR Software 7

    3.4. The Growth of Social VR 7

    3.5. Emerging Applications in Social Work 7

    3.6. VR's Compelling Future 8

4. Case Studies: Witnessing Change Through VR 9

    4.1. Case Study 1: Empathy Training for Social Workers 9

    4.2. Case Study 2: Using VR for Trauma Therapy 10

    4.3. Case Study 3: Immersive Learning in Child Services 10

    4.4. Case Study 4: Building Community Resilience Through VR . . 11

5. VR and Empathy: Bridging Emotional Distances 12

    5.1. The Science of Empathy and VR 12

    5.2. VR Platforms Empowering Empathy 13

    5.3. Empathy Amplification in Social Work 13

    5.4. Future Projections 14

    5.5. In Conclusion 14

6. Revisiting Therapy: VR in Mental Health 16

    6.1. The Emergence of VR in Therapy 16

    6.2. The Integration of VR into Therapy 17

6.3. VR Therapy for Anxiety Disorders 17

6.4. VR Therapy for Post-Traumatic Stress Disorder (PTSD) 18

6.5. VR Therapy for Psychotic Disorders 18

6.6. Potential Challenges of VR in Therapy 18

6.7. The Road Ahead 19

7. Immersive Education and Training for Social Workers 20

7.1. The Nuance of Virtual Reality 20

7.2. Expanding Educational Techniques 21

7.3. Real-world Simulations: Benefits and Drawbacks 21

7.4. VR and Ethical Consideraions 21

7.5. Future Projections 22

7.6. Conclusion 22

8. The Roles of VR in Crisis Intervention 24

8.1. VR as a Therapeutic Solution 24

8.2. Transforming Social Worker Training 25

8.3. Innovative Tools for Law Enforcement 25

8.4. Potential Barriers and Looking Forward 26

9. Ethical Considerations in Applying VR to Social Work 27

9.1. A New Ethical Landscape 27

9.2. Privacy and Confidentiality 28

9.3. Emotional Vulnerability 28

9.4. The Need for New Guidelines 28

9.5. Case Studies as Guides 29

9.6. Regulatory Perspectives and Legal Principles 29

10. Inclusion and Accessibility in VR: Challenges and Solutions 31

10.1. Potential Hurdles to Accessibility 31

10.2. Rethinking Accessibility 32

10.3. Overcoming Technological Hurdles 32

10.4. Addressing Humanistic Hurdles 32

10.5. VR and Inclusion 33

10.6. Case Study: The VR Wheelchair Project 33

10.7. Navigating the Future 33

11. Guiding the Future: The Next Frontier of VR in Social Work 35

11.1. Immersive Experience: The Heart of VR 35

11.2. The Revolution of VR Therapy 36

11.3. VR: Bridging Social Gaps 36

11.4. Training and Education in Social Work: A New Paradigm . . 37

11.5. Challenges and Considerations 37

11.6. Shaping the Future of Social Work 38

Chapter 1. Introduction

In this forward-thinking Special Report, we delve into the remarkably transformative landscape of Virtual Reality (VR) within the realm of social work, shedding light on how this immersive technology is reshaping and enhancing our ability to effectuate positive change in the lives of individuals and communities. As VR enters the fray, it presents us with an entirely new set of tools that offer unprecedented levels of interactivity and engagement. This is not a hyper-technical savant's guide, but a highly accessible exploration ripe with compelling case studies, expert insights, and discerning projections about the future. Brimming with verve and enthusiasm, this report provides a practical, down-to-earth viewpoint that will resonate with both seasoned social practitioners and curious technology enthusiasts. Prepare to be motivated, enlightened, and captivated—and to envision a captivating new future for social work as we know it. Invest in your copy today to gain an indispensable edge in this burgeoning field.

Chapter 2. The Dawn of Virtual Reality in Social Work

The advent of Virtual Reality (VR) marks an innovative era within social work, offering thrilling potential for enhancing the efficacy and reach of interventions. Although still in its relative infancy, the application of VR in social work is rapidly gaining recognition for its versatility and engaging nature.

2.1. The Advent of VR and its Integration in Social Work

The genesis of VR was rooted in the realm of gaming and entertainment, lauded for its capacity to create captivating and immersive experiences. Over time, technology advancements have facilitated its emergence into numerous other sectors, including education, healthcare and, now, social work.

VR's integration into social work is undeniably transformative. Simulating real-life scenarios in controlled environments can be particularly potent for developing empathy, understanding, and insight, crucial for social workers. VR not merely mirrors the course of action in the physical, 'real' world, but also enhances interaction, offering a novel platform for learning, intervention, and skill enhancement.

2.2. Evolving Applications of VR in Social Work

Initially, VR's applications within social work were primarily geared towards enhancing professionals' training and skill-development. Users would engage with character avatars in virtual scenarios, practicing their communicational and problem-solving skills.

In more recent times, VR's usage has evolved, diversifying across various dimensions of social work. VR technology is being employed for client-directed interventions. These are designed to aid individuals in managing issues like substance abuse, anxiety disorders, and post-traumatic stress. VR acts as a medium to retell their stories, revisiting difficult scenarios safely, enabling therapists to guide them through the healing process.

Another realm is facilitating virtual home visits. Geographical restrictions are nullified as social workers can visit a client's home within this virtual space, an innovation that is unsurpassably invaluable amid worldwide travel restrictions resultant of the COVID-19 pandemic.

Finally, VR is being used to develop empathy and understanding in the context of anti-racist and cultural competence training. Here, individuals are submerged in experiences that reveal their biases and prejudices, providing them insights, realizations otherwise unattainable.

2.3. Extant Research on VR in Social Work

To date, several studies reinforce the efficacy of VR within social work. In a study by Dyer et al. (2018), a VR-based training module improved child welfare workers' observational skills and informed decision-making.

Likewise, Baceviciute (2018) used VR to elicit empathy amongst social work students, presuming that literature and lectures often fall short of this pivotal goal. Because of VR, students could experience the perspective of a struggling single mother in a realistic scenario—receiving first-hand insights.

Although the body of research is still growing, preliminary evidence clearly points to VR's potential as an effective tool for social work interventions and training.

2.4. Challenges and Limitations

Despite VR's burgeoning benefits, it is accompanied with several challenges and limitations. Accessibility is a paramount concern. Not all social agencies possess the funds necessary for cutting-edge technology investment. Also, the issues of cyber safety, confidentiality breaches, and privacy invasion are yet to be fully addressed.

Additionally, there's an absence of a comprehensive, evidence-based guide on how to best utilize VR within social work contexts—to guarantee its effectiveness, matching the right kind of VR to the right kind of problem.

2.5. The Future of VR in Social Work

The future course of VR within social work seems remarkably promising. The greatest potential lies in enhancing areas of professional training, client interventions, and research.

As we continue to explore the applications of VR, the technology's full potential in social work will eventually unfold, shaping new paths and paving the way for possibly the most exciting chapter in the field's evolution.

In conclusion, the dawn of VR in social work augurs astoundingly well. The potent tool facilitates immersive, engaging, and transformative encounters and interventions that were unthinkable just a few years ago. Hold onto your headsets: the future of social work looks virtually impressive!

Chapter 3. Decoding Virtual Reality: Context and Mechanics

To begin, we ought to understand that Virtual Reality (VR) is an advanced form of interactive technology that renders users a 3D computer-generated environment, which they can explore and interact with. The user can immerse within this environment, introspectively viewing it from an occupant's, rather than spectator's perspective, making the experience indistinguishably real from physical reality. VR effectively tricks the brain into believing we are somewhere we are not. A host of complex technologies go into creating this illusion.

3.1. Understanding the Technology Behind VR

One of the foundational aspects of VR technology is the Head-Mounted Display (HMD). HMDs are worn on the head like a helmet, with screens placed in front of the eyes to provide a stereoscopic 3D view. The HMDs come equipped with sensors tracking the movement of the user's head, ensuring that the image on the screen complies with her/his line of sight. HDR, Full HD, OLED technology, and other breakthroughs have made significant improvements in HMD displays, leading to higher resolution and an increasingly realistic VR experience with more detailed environments.

Another key piece of hardware required to create VR environments is the connectivity module. Historically, VR systems relied on wired connections to transmit data from sensors and transmit visual information to the headset. However, recent advances have enabled wireless connections, allowing for untethered VR experiences with significantly improved freedom of movement and accessibility.

Sound, too, plays a vital role in making the VR experience more real, which can be achieved through stereo sound systems. Applying principles of psychoacoustics to map sounds based on their position from the listener makes them perceive audio sources in 3D space.

3.2. The Role of Interactivity

Interactivity is the cornerstone of VR experiences. While conventional forms of media provide a static, outside-looking-in viewpoint, VR enables an immersive environment in which the viewer can actively contribute to the narrative. Interactivity is managed through a range of different systems, including motion capture, eye-tracking technology, and controllers.

In VR, motion capture technology tracks the user's bodily movements and transitions them into VR, allowing the user's inputs to influence the VR experience directly. Imagine climbing a mountain, reaching out to grab something, or running from danger—all enacted within the confines of your living room but replicated within the VR world.

Eye-tracking technology is another essential aspect of VR interactivity. VR systems with integrated eye-tracking capabilities can help the user to focus on specific objects or areas in the VR environment, creating natural and realistic experiences.

Controllers, on the other hand, can be handheld or worn on the body, facilitating interaction with the VR environment. These can also deliver haptic feedback, allowing the player to receive physical responses like the feel of a button being pressed, a ball being thrown, or an enemy strike.

3.3. The State of VR Software

The VR environment is created through sophisticated software applications that render 3D environments. The details, interactions, and physics of the VR environment are all designed and managed using this software. Libraries enable developers to create dynamic, interactive VR experiences complete with physics, sounds, and lighting effects.

3.4. The Growth of Social VR

Social reality is a burgeoning field within VR wherein multiple users can interact within the same VR environment in real-time. This concept falls under the shared spaced VR model which focuses on encouraging social connections. It offers the potential to create novel, empathetic experiences, thereby signifying its relevance to social work.

3.5. Emerging Applications in Social Work

Within the precincts of social work, VR has an enormous potential to bring about marked change. It can act as a conduit to facilitate empathy by placing users directly into the shoes of those experiencing life's challenges, generating a perspective change and fostering understanding. As we further decode the potential of VR, one thing has been established beyond doubt: it's not merely a new tool but it heralds a paradigm shift. With understanding and thoughtful application, it could redefine our experiences, interactions, and ultimately, our societies.

3.6. VR's Compelling Future

While we have only explored the tip of the VR iceberg, the exciting future of this technology and its potential applications in social work is beyond compelling. Continued developments in VR hardware, software, and interaction methods promise engaging and transformative experiences that will revolutionize the manner in which we perceive and interact with the world. The social work realm is perched on the brink of this change. With the power of VR, the potential to effectuate positive change in the lives of individuals and communities is colossal. We're just getting started on this journey, and it's going to be one fascinating ride!

Chapter 4. Case Studies: Witnessing Change Through VR

The awakening of a fresh technological dawn with Virtual Reality (VR) promises an era of impactful interventions in the social work sphere. With a series of pioneering case studies, we undertake an exploratory journey, delving into the transformative immersions of VR that epitomize the future of social work.

4.1. Case Study 1: Empathy Training for Social Workers

At the heart of every successful social work intervention is empathy—a fundamental understanding and sharing of the feelings and perspectives of individuals in distress. Traditional modes of imparting this essential skill have included lectures, textbooks, and group discussions, often proving insufficient to instigate the necessary empathetic resonance.

Enter VR, and the Empathy Amplifier project. Launched in 2019 by Birmingham University, this groundbreaking initiative explored the efficacy of VR in enhancing empathy among trainee social workers. The project involved immersive VR experiences simulating the lived experiences of homeless individuals, children in foster care, and survivors of domestic abuse.

Post-program evaluations highlighted VR's capacity to stir profound emotional engagement, thereby promoting enhanced empathy. Participants reported a seismic shift in their understanding and empathy towards the presented cases, substantiating the immense potential of VR as a game-changer in social work training.

4.2. Case Study 2: Using VR for Trauma Therapy

The haunting aftermath of trauma often eludes conventional therapeutic approaches. VR's capacity to create safe, controlled environments for exposure therapy has shown promise in helping trauma survivors regain control and facilitating their healing journeys.

Project Brave, initiated by a non-profit in Denver, Colorado, has been leveraging VR technology to treat individuals affected by traumatic experiences. Through their innovative approach, clients gradually face their fears and anxieties in a VR environment, directly confronting what once seemed impossible in a safe space.

Over 80% of Project Brave's clients, after undergoing their VR-facilitated exposure therapy, report a substantial reduction in PTSD symptoms. These strides forward underscore VR's powerful role as a therapeutic tool that embodies promise, healing, and transformation.

4.3. Case Study 3: Immersive Learning in Child Services

Virtual reality presents an arsenal of tools that boost experiential learning, particularly in the child services niche. The Virtual Home Project spearheaded by the University of Kent in the UK, created a compelling virtual environment that allowed trainee social workers to experience and understand the day-to-day reality of children living amid deprivation.

In the virtual space, participants are faced with the stark realities of poverty, witnessing firsthand the detrimental impact on children's development and welfare. The immersive exposure gives a jarring realness to the socioeconomic barriers impoverished families face, fostering a greater understanding that transcends traditional textbook knowledge.

The project showed an 85% increase in participant empathy, with trainee social workers self-reporting a refreshed outlook on their roles. For those involved, VR has managed to bridge the knowledge-experience gap, bolting experiential learning to the blueprint of social work education.

4.4. Case Study 4: Building Community Resilience Through VR

The VRommunity Initiative by the Australian Council of Social Welfare focused on fostering better community resilience to deal with natural disasters. Through highly realistic VR simulations of bushfires or floods, residents could prepare for such occurrences. Users learn to make difficult decisions under pressure and appreciate the merit of pre-disaster planning.

Through this immersive learning, the VRommunity Initiative has successfully helped the communities foster crisis resilience. Households demonstrate more readily-available disaster management plans, and community-specific mobilization strategies have evolved, testifying to the power and practicality of VR-led engagement.

These case studies, where VR technology has been applied to reshape social work, underscore this digital Renaissance's power in our profession. VR provides us with unprecedented tools that offer immersive, engaging solutions, possessing great potential to revolutionize the way social workers learn, practice, and effect change in individuals and communities. The burgeoning interplay between VR and social work, as demonstrated in these case studies, offers a glimpse into a thrilling and hopeful horizon that promises to reshape the sphere of social work forever.

Chapter 5. VR and Empathy: Bridging Emotional Distances

VR technology holds substantial potential to strengthen the empathetic bonds between social workers and their clients. This chapter explores the intersection of empathy and VR, deciphering how they collectively enhance the understanding of individual perspectives, emotions, and experiences.

5.1. The Science of Empathy and VR

Empathy, at its core, pertains to the acknowledgment and understanding of someone else's emotional condition. It is a critical aspect of effective social work as it fosters relationships of trust, facilitates two-way communication, and often steers the course of interventions.

VR, on the other hand, has recently emerged as a transformative tool for delivering real-life experiences through immersive, multi-sensory 3D environments. VR provides an unparalleled platform to witness first-hand the circumstances, challenges, and realities faced by others.

When these two worlds collide, something extraordinary happens: the birth of a nurturing crossroad where social workers can vividly comprehend their clients' emotional foundation, in addition to the relevant socio-economic backgrounds.

According to Stanford University's Virtual Human Interaction Lab, utilizing VR for empathy training showed a 27% increase in users' empathetic responses. By stepping into different virtual shoes, it becomes possible to grasp life from myriad perspectives previously unseen or unimaginable.

5.2. VR Platforms Empowering Empathy

Numerous VR platforms have actively adopted and cultivated empathy arenas:

1. Walking in Another's Virtual Shoes: Here, the user is virtually placed in different life scenarios, experiencing diverse socio-economic and cultural conditions. One notable example is "Being Homeless," a project by the Stanford Lab, which depicts the harsh realities of homelessness and challenges associated with it.

2. Virtual Therapy: VR therapy session intend to simulate emotional and mental health issues accurately. Apps such as "Fear of Heights," let the user experience phobias and related anxieties, fostering a deeper understanding of those coping with these conditions daily.

3. Humans of VR: It's a process of learning human stories through VR technology inside-out, by stepping into virtual recreations of real individuals' lives who have faced or are facing specific challenges, such as racial discrimination, isolation, loneliness, or PTSD.

5.3. Empathy Amplification in Social Work

Social work often deals with individuals and communities coping with intense situations of distress. VR's potent ability to facilitate empathy can thus notably transform how social workers understand and assist their clients.

- Virtual Reality Exposure Therapy (VRET): VRET is a therapeutic technique that uses VR to treat anxiety disorders, including PTSD. It exposes clients to the triggers in a safe, controlled environment, thus helping them manage their symptoms better. VRET exemplifies an empathy-driven VR application where the therapist can comprehend what triggers a person's anxiety, and subsequently curate individualized coping strategies.

- Cultural Competency: VR can help social workers understand and negotiate the cultural dimensions of empathy by providing immersive experiences of different cultures, ethnicities, and lifestyles drastically different from their own. This can help reduce cultural biases and foster a more inclusive approach to social work.

5.4. Future Projections

While we're at a nascent stage in integrating VR into social work, the potential is immense. As the accessibility and affordability of VR technology improve, we can envision a larger adoption rate in the realm of social work.

The potential for empathy training and education is staggering. VR can be seamlessly incorporated into university curricula for social work, causing a paradigm shift in the teaching and learning of empathy, thus shaping more balanced, empathetic professionals.

VR-based empathy tools can also be useful in policy-making. Policymakers can gain a deeper understanding of marginalised communities and design better, more inclusive policies.

5.5. In Conclusion

The intersection of VR and empathy is a transformative nexus in social work, offering opportunities for an insightful emotional journey into the lives and experiences of those they serve. As an innovative and powerful tool, VR stands to empower, strengthen, and invigorate the realm of social work. It promises to bring about substantial shifts in the way we understand emotions, human suffering, and the basis of our shared human experience.

While challenges remain, including cost constraints and acceptance among older practitioners, the potential benefits far outweigh the drawbacks. As this exciting new frontier gains momentum and becomes further finessed, social work stands on the brink of a revolutionary transition that could redefine its sphere entirely.

Embracing these developments with an open heart and a curious mind, social work practitioners can step into a future where physical presence no longer dictates the boundaries of emotional understanding and compassion. The possibilities are boundless and thrillingly transformative, carrying remarkable potential to shape the future of social work. "Immerse to emerge," they say; indeed, VR is the rising tide sure to take social work along to vistas of unparalleled empathy and support.

Chapter 6. Revisiting Therapy: VR in Mental Health

Advancements in technology have opened up infinite possibilities in a myriad of disciplines, and psychology and mental health are no exceptions. The amalgamation of virtual reality (VR) and therapy can now provide compelling solutions to previously intractable problems, which this entry expounds in great detail.

6.1. The Emergence of VR in Therapy

The journey of virtual reality as a therapeutic tool began in the early 1990s. However, back then, the technology was not only expensive but also cumbersome, limiting its accessibility. Fast forward to today, the situation is entirely different. VR headsets are now more affordable and are constantly being improved for user experience, making VR a viable option for psychologists and therapists to explore. The realm of virtual reality has opened doors to new and innovative therapeutic interventions, particularly in the field of mental health.

VR as a therapeutic tool is often used in Exposure Therapy, a technique that exposes patients repeatedly to a feared object or traumatic memory in a safe setting, thereby reducing the fear response. By creating immersive, controllable, and customizable environments, VR has revolutionized exposure therapy by providing therapists with an incredible degree of control and flexibility.

6.2. The Integration of VR into Therapy

Before delving into the application of VR in various mental health conditions, it is essential to understand how VR integrates into therapy sessions. Therapy using VR typically involves three stages: introduction, exposure, and debriefing.

In the introduction stage, the therapist explains the nature and purpose of the VR session, allaying any fears the patient may harbor regarding the technology. During the exposure stage, the patient wears a VR headset and is immersed in a virtual environment that addresses their specific mental health issue. Lastly, during debriefing, the therapist and the patient discuss the experience and the emotions that arose. It constitutes a critical part of the therapy as it enables the patient to consolidate their learning and make meaning of their experiences.

6.3. VR Therapy for Anxiety Disorders

When it comes to anxiety disorders, exposure therapy is a time-tested and evidence-based therapeutic intervention. However, practical implementation can be challenging, especially in situations where the feared object or situation cannot be realistically or safely recreated. This is where VR steps in, enabling therapists to create controllable and realistic scenarios that mimic real-life situations causing anxiety.

For instance, VR therapy has proven beneficial in treating phobias such as fear of flying, where a realistic flight simulation can be created. Similarly, people who struggle with social anxiety can practice interacting in a variety of social settings without experiencing real-world consequences.

6.4. VR Therapy for Post-Traumatic Stress Disorder (PTSD)

Another area where VR has shown great promise is in the treatment of PTSD. Here, VR is used to create a representation of the traumatic event, allowing the therapist to control the intensity of the situation so that the patient can confront and process the traumatic memory safely.

Over the years, numerous studies have demonstrated the efficacy of VR in treating PTSD. Emotional engagement in a safe, controlled environment appears to enhance the effect of exposure therapy in ways that traditional methods might not achieve.

6.5. VR Therapy for Psychotic Disorders

Psychotic disorders, such as schizophrenia, can lead to hallucinations and delusions that disconnect the individual from reality. There is emerging evidence to suggest that VR can be used to understand better and treat such disorders. By creating virtual avatars that mirror the audio-visual hallucinations experienced by these patients, therapists can work with them to address their symptoms in a controlled environment.

6.6. Potential Challenges of VR in Therapy

Despite its evident advantages, the integration of VR into therapy does not come without potential pitfalls. First, using VR requires adequate training for the therapist to provide a beneficial experience for the patient. Second, certain patients may experience cybersickness, a condition similar to motion sickness caused by navigating a virtual environment. Finally, the lack of guidelines and regulations around VR use in therapy, coupled with data privacy concerns, adds an extra layer of complexity.

6.7. The Road Ahead

The story of VR in therapy has just begun. Future iterations of the technology promise to include features like biofeedback, where virtual scenarios change in response to the patient's physiological reactions, enhancing the therapeutic process.

The potential benefits of VR in therapy are difficult to overstate – it allows therapists to stride into the minds of their patients, creating experiences that can catalyze profound change and healing, all controlled, measured, and manipulated in ways traditional therapy has only dreamed of. Yet, as with all technologies, careful and thoughtful implementation is key to using VR to its fullest potential.

This chapter has aimed at outlining how VR technology is carving a niche for itself in mental health therapy. The endless possibilities of VR's integration with therapeutic interventions promise a better future for mental health support, bringing empathy, engagement, and effectiveness to a whole new level. As we continue to explore and understand the applications of VR in mental health, we can feel hopeful and excited about the array of possibilities it presents.

Chapter 7. Immersive Education and Training for Social Workers

The transformative potential of Virtual Reality (VR) in social work education and training cannot be overstated. With its immersive characteristics, VR bolsters the learning process by offering realistic, practical, and interactive experiences. This enables social workers to cultivate and refine their skillset in a controlled environment before venturing into the field.

7.1. The Nuance of Virtual Reality

VR's essence lies in its immersive quality. More than just a collection of pixelated landscapes or digital characters, VR enables users to interact with a computer-simulated world using sensors and input devices. Depending on the sophistication of the setup, users can see, hear, and even feel simulated elements, turning the VR environment into an experiential platform.

Several types of VR exist, from non-immersive simulations, where users navigate digital realms using a computer and keyboard, to fully immersive systems, where users don head-mounted displays and data gloves to move freely within the virtual environment.

These seamless transitions between the real and virtual worlds make VR an extremely powerful tool for learning. By allowing realistic role playing, VR helps the learner internalize concepts and strategies.

7.2. Expanding Educational Techniques

Crucial to social work education is the acquisition and application of knowledge about human behavior, societal structures, and relevant policies. While conventional teaching methods, including lectures, case studies, and discussions are effective, there is a growing recognition of the benefits of experiential learning through VR.

VR-based simulations provide authentic and complex scenarios that social work practitioners might encounter in their careers. This allows them to practice skills such as empathy, problem-solving, and decision-making in a low-stakes environment. Whether it's managing a challenging interaction with a client or navigating dense bureaucracy, VR offers a practical, hands-on learning experience.

7.3. Real-world Simulations: Benefits and Drawbacks

One of the most significant benefits of VR simulations in social work education is the realism it provides. VR can replicate scenarios involving individuals, families, communities, or organizations with a level of detail and complexity that conventional case studies or role-playing exercises cannot.

However, there is the risk that over-reliance on VR could reduce human interaction, a fundamental aspect of social work. Balancing VR training with traditional educational methods can foster a more holistic learning experience.

7.4. VR and Ethical Consideraions

Additionally, VR-based education and training must consider ethical implications. Virtual simulations featuring difficult or distressing situations may cause emotional distress to the learner. Hence, proper educational design and ethics guidelines must be put in place.

7.5. Future Projections

As VR technology advances and becomes more affordable, expect to see its increased incorporation in social work education. Consequently, new pedagogical models may emerge that meld traditional teaching methods with VR-based experiential learning. The effect of these developments on educational outcomes, practitioner competence, and clients' wellbeing will be fascinating to observe.

7.6. Conclusion

Immersive VR-based education and training offer a promising avenue for enriching social work education. By turning classrooms into digital laboratories where authentic and complex scenarios can be explored, VR has the potential to deepen learner engagement, enhance skill acquisition, and ultimately, prepare more proficient practitioners.

The road towards integrating VR into social work education, however, is not without its challenges, especially concerning ethical considerations. Regardless of these hurdles, the benefits outweigh the drawbacks. It's clear that with thoughtful and strategic implementation, VR can transform the landscape of social work education, yielding positive outcomes for learners, professionals, and communities.

VR isn't merely the future of social work education; indeed, the future is here. As we move forward, we should be ready to embrace this technology's transformative power, while remaining grounded in the fundamental values of social work. After all, VR, in all its glory, is but a tool to help us serve individuals and communities better. The essence, spirit, and goal of social work remain firmly in the realm of the human touch.

Chapter 8. The Roles of VR in Crisis Intervention

The reality of our multifaceted society today bears an urgent demand for mediums that enhance our approach towards crisis intervention. With the advent of Virtual Reality (VR), the boundaries of possibility have been enticingly stretched, enabling us to explore new vistas in a variety of sectors, crisis intervention being a key one. As an influential factor in social work and with considerable potential to reform crisis intervention, VR demands a comprehensive study, which will be undertaken in the ensuing analysis.

8.1. VR as a Therapeutic Solution

The immersive nature of VR lends it potency as a therapeutic tool. VR's capability to construct a controlled yet realistic environment offers therapists a safe environment to replicate crises, determine triggers, and develop coping mechanisms.

A case study illustrating this involves the treatment of Post-Traumatic Stress Disorder (PTSD) in veterans. The patient, fully immersed in a war-like scenario, is exposed to elements triggering their trauma. Though seemingly counter-intuitive, this exposure helps them confront their fears rather than escape them. Herein lies a central tenet of trauma-focused therapy – facing one's fears rather than seeking to avoid them.

Another exemplary study involves agoraphobia patients undergoing virtual exposure therapy. Patients find themselves in simulated public spaces—complete with crowds and ambient noise—that raise their anxiety levels, a critical step towards therapy. Incremental improvements are measured and managed, enabling progressive desensitization and behavioral adaptation.

8.2. Transforming Social Worker Training

Another crucial role of VR in crisis intervention lies in improving the training provided to social workers. By presenting a broad spectrum of crisis scenarios in hyper-realistic, controlled environments, VR facilitates more nuanced and practice-driven training, thereby enhancing the effectiveness of support during real-world interventions.

One example is the creation of VR training scenarios for social workers dealing with high-risk adolescent cases involving substance abuse. These scenarios present challenging family dynamics and environmental experiences that social workers can encounter, providing them with the opportunity to trial various intervention procedures. This hands-on learning experience promotes a deeper understanding of the crisis—the first step towards a more empathetic and successful intervention.

8.3. Innovative Tools for Law Enforcement

Law enforcement agencies are not typically considered in discussions surrounding social work, yet they cannot be discounted in crisis intervention. By incorporating VR, these organizations can develop more sensitive and tactful approaches.

Evidence of this innovation arrives from programs designed to train police officers to respond more appropriately to individuals dealing with mental health crises. In a VR environment, officers experience simulations involving potential real-life scenarios. The realistic simulations, combined with scenario-specific tips and coaching, yield a more empathetic, patient-focused response from law enforcement officers, drastically reducing the risk of escalation.

8.4. Potential Barriers and Looking Forward

While VR's potential in crisis intervention is vast, potential challenges arise. The most obvious relates to resource availability—VR requires technology, expertise, and investment, which might be beyond the reach of many communities. There's the ancillary challenge of acceptance—both from providers and those receiving support—who may push back against this "foreign" method of support.

However, overcoming these barriers seems achievable when weighed against the transformative potential of VR in crisis intervention. VR promises a journey towards compassionate, inclusive, and innovative social support. Further research, stakeholder engagement, and sensitivity towards the peculiarities of individual communities will be instrumental in navigating this journey.

In conclusion, the transformative potential of VR in the realms of crisis intervention and social work is beginning to unveil itself. As a tool for therapy, a vehicle for training social workers with a pragmatic approach, and a transformative instrument for law enforcement, VR can reshape the way we engage with crises, act towards them, and finally, intervene effectively. The way forward lies in continued exploration, investigation and adaption of this immersive technology for the betterment of our societal mechanisms.

Chapter 9. Ethical Considerations in Applying VR to Social Work

Just as the integration of virtual reality into social work presents unmatched possibilities to improve communities and individual lives, it also calls forth a new array of ethical considerations. Attempting to uphold professional principles and regulations within this nascent framework is akin to navigating uncharted waters, necessitating the utmost vigilance, foresight, and ingenuity to confront the challenges that inevitably arise.

9.1. A New Ethical Landscape

Virtual reality's ascent in the sphere of social work invites the formation of a new ethical landscape. Immersive digital environments can mimic real-world experiences with such fidelity that they touch upon personal and communal sensitivities. VR implementations can profoundly alter our understanding of privacy, foster emotional vulnerability, or risk the exploitation of participants. Thereby, a thoughtful approach to translating real-world ethical considerations into VR contexts becomes crucial.

Among the foremost dilemmas involved in adapting VR to social work are informed consent, privacy, and confidentiality. While these foundational elements of professional ethics remain unchanged in their essence, they take on unique complexities in the digital domain.

Traditionally, we understand informed consent as the foregrounding premise for any client-service provider interaction. Clients must be given a comprehensive understanding of the nature of the planned intervention, its objectives, potential risks, and possible alternatives. However, translating this principle into a VR experience raises a host of questions: How do we adequately convey the sensory depth and emotional impact of experiences that exist beyond our collective understanding? Is it possible to fully warn individuals about the potential distress they may encounter during unfamiliar virtual experiences?

9.2. Privacy and Confidentiality

Privacy and confidentiality, too, are imbued with fresh nuances in VR scenarios. While VR applications may record only anonymized data or manipulated digital representations of clients, the intimate nature of these interactions might nonetheless lead to perceived or actual invasions of privacy. The comprehensive records of movement, interaction, and expression that VR systems might compile can potentially be viewed as intrusive documentation of highly personal information. Consequently, practitioners must prioritize the development of secure data storage and handling procedures that assuage potential privacy concerns.

9.3. Emotional Vulnerability

Emotional vulnerability represents another significant ethical challenge in VR social work. Due to the profoundly immersive nature of VR, individuals may unexpectedly encounter distressing circumstances or discover latent sensitivities during VR therapies. It consequently raises concerns about the practitioner's ability to adequately monitor, manage, or alleviate such challenges without causing further emotional trauma.

9.4. The Need for New Guidelines

Given these unique ethical considerations intrinsic to VR technologies in social work, there is a pressing need for new guidelines and principles. To develop these, social workers, ethicists, and technology designers need to collaborate, fusing their particular perspectives and experiences. It's pivotal to approach these challenges with a spirit of innovation and adaptation, translating time-honored ethical principles into new-eon forms that account for the unique contexts and capabilities that VR brings to bear.

9.5. Case Studies as Guides

Case studies of other sectors where VR has been deployed, such as healthcare, education, and entertainment, may offer helpful precedents and insights. Importantly, the cultivation of ongoing dialogue with professionals in these and other relevant fields can foster a richly informed and nuanced understanding of best practices for ethical VR implementation.

9.6. Regulatory Perspectives and Legal Principles

Embedding VR into social work also invokes regulatory and legal considerations. Current professional standards and legal principles may be ill-equipped to accommodate novel scenarios precipitated by VR technologies. Consequently, an in-depth exploration and possible revision of professional regulatory standards and legal principles might prove requisite.

The next stride in crafting symbiosis between ethical values and VR in social work is to create a supportive environment for dialogue, testing, and experimentation. Building a community of practice where professionals from diverse sectors share their experiences and insights, compile and interpret empirical data, and examine ethical dilemmas under varying real-world contexts, could drive forward evidence-based ethical practices.

This groundbreaking application of VR in social work represents a promising, yet challenging frontier. To wield it thoughtfully and ethically, we must contend with the novel ethical challenges it introduces. The rewards of this endeavor could be transformative, leading the way to a future where technological and social advancements harmonize to enrich communities and individual lives, guided by ethical discernment.

Chapter 10. Inclusion and Accessibility in VR: Challenges and Solutions

As we delve into the uncharted territories of VR integration within social services, it's paramount to address the seemingly elephant in the room - Inclusion and Accessibility. VR technology, in all its marvel, also brings forth a set of unique challenges not previously encountered in conventional methodologies, prompting practitioners to redesign their approach to their practices to cater to these emergent needs. Conversely, VR also offers hope through creative solutions that fling open the doors of accessibility to those hitherto disenfranchised.

10.1. Potential Hurdles to Accessibility

The primary hurdles in VR integration emerge in twofold - technological and humanistic. Technological hurdles are prevalent and revolve around components like hardware requirements, software compatibility, and internet accessibility. Not all clients might possess the necessary gadgetry or the technical skills to operate them right off the bat.

Similarly, humanistic hurdles deal with VR's inherent characteristics. While immersive experiences can be riveting, they can also be disorientating or overwhelming for some users, especially those new to the system.

10.2. Rethinking Accessibility

To circumvent these obstacles, we have to rethink accessibility in the VR context. Conventionally, accessibility refers to the ability to use, navigate, and understand services or systems. With VR, however, we are dealing with three-dimensional virtual spaces that require different ways of traversing and understanding. This extends the notion of accessibility beyond physical disabilities to include cognitive, socioeconomic, and even geographical considerations.

10.3. Overcoming Technological Hurdles

While we can't comphrehensively eliminate technological hurdles overnight, we can lessen their impact. With the endeavor to make VR a commonly accepted tool, manufacturers have begun offering cost-effective VR viewing devices that require no more than a smartphone. Furthermore, organizations can explore the provision of VR equipment to those in need, taking inspiration from initiatives like Project ECHO which helped to democratize access to medical expertise by using technology.

In terms of software, VR applications are being developed with a nod to intuitiveness, reducing the requirements of technical adeptness. Organizations might also consider comprehensive tutorials and technical support to further allay the fears of the technically challenged.

10.4. Addressing Humanistic Hurdles

Addressing humanistic hurdles requires a more nuanced and delicate approach. It requires acclimatizing users to VR environments gradually, starting with less intense experiences and incrementally increasing complexity. Regular breaks should be introduced to prevent simulator sickness associated with prolonged exposure.

Additionally, it's essential to work in tandem with psychologists and professionals to ensure the tools used promote therapeutic engagement instead of causing unnecessary distress.

10.5. VR and Inclusion

While consideration of challenges is important, we must not lose sight of VR's potential in enhancing inclusion. By transcending the boundaries of physical limitations, VR can provide valuable experiences to those who might otherwise be excluded. Those bedridden or geographically distant can be virtually present and engage meaningfully. VR can also be customized to meet the needs of those facing cognitive difficulties. For example, a virtual environment can be modified to cater to visually impaired individuals by increasing contrast or removing graphical clutter.

10.6. Case Study: The VR Wheelchair Project

An inspiring case in point is 'The VR Wheelchair Project.' Driven by an ambition to make VR experiences accessible to wheelchair users, specialized hardware was developed to emulate wheelchair movements within the VR environment, thus removing barriers to accessibility and promoting inclusive gaming and social interactions.

10.7. Navigating the Future

Looking forward, the onus is on us to ensure that VR serves as a tool for enhancing social work rather than impeding it. The challenges are significant, but not insurmountable, and the opportunities for innovation are vast. As VR continues to evolve, we can expect the hurdles to dissipate while the benefits only become more pronounced. Through continuous learning and consistent effort, the realm of VR in social work is on track to become more accessible and inclusive than ever.

Chapter 11. Guiding the Future: The Next Frontier of VR in Social Work

As the sphere of Virtual Reality (VR) expands and evolves, we stand on the precipice of unprecedented transformation within the field of social work. This technology, which was once relegated to the realms of science fiction, is now a tangible tool that can be harnessed to foster profound change and facilitate unparalleled connection between social workers and the communities they serve.

11.1. Immersive Experience: The Heart of VR

At its core, VR technology is about immersion - creating an interactive and engaging environment that pulls the participant into a realm different from their own immediate physical environment. VR's immersive qualities can serve multiple functions in the field of social work. Let's explore exactly how.

First, it can provide social workers with an empathetic understanding of the individuals and communities they serve. Rather than hearing or reading about the circumstances that surround an individual, VR can allow social workers to see, hear, and interact within these environments or situations, effectively 'walking a mile in their shoes'.

Imagine, for instance, the plight of an elderly individual. But now, think of experiencing their world through VR—attempting to navigate a house with restricted mobility, attempting tasks with compromised dexterity or eyesight, or experiencing the psychological impact of isolation. This 'immersive empathy' could revolutionize the way social workers understand and respond to the individual's circumstances.

Second, VR can enable social workers to assess environments, families, and communities remotely. This form of virtual 'home visitation' could greatly extend the reach of social workers, facilitating support to communities that may previously have been inaccessible due to distance, safety considerations, or limited resources.

11.2. The Revolution of VR Therapy

Alongside these practical applications, VR is also opening up new strategies for therapeutic intervention. VR therapy mixes immersive virtual environments with therapeutic processes, and has shown significant potentials in various fields, such as:

- Anxiety Disorders: By using exposure therapy through VR, individuals can confront and manage their fears in a controlled environment.
- PTSD: Virtual reality exposure therapy (VRET) can recreate traumatic scenarios, helping individuals learn how to better cope and process their experiences.
- Autism Spectrum Disorders: VR can help in improving social interaction and communication skills by offering safe and controlled social scenarios.

The above represent just the tip of the iceberg. While further research and development are needed, the initial outcomes are certainly promising.

11.3. VR: Bridging Social Gaps

By utilizing VR, social work can also foster understanding and bridge gaps within communities. For instance, people can virtually step into each others' lives and experiences—promoting empathy, dispelling stereotypes and addressing prejudices.

Consider a community fractured along racial, economic, or cultural lines. A well-designed VR experience could help individuals understand the challenges faced by different groups within their community, thereby fostering greater understanding and promoting unity.

11.4. Training and Education in Social Work: A New Paradigm

VR also offers transformative possibilities across the gamut of social work education. Virtual role-playing scenarios can provide students with practical experiences that closely mirror the reality.

Imagine a training scenario wherein students interact with a virtual child suffering from abuse or a family in crisis. The experience would allow them to test their responses, make mistakes, learn, and adapt in a fail-safe environment. Such virtual scenarios can be repeated and adapted, catering to a variety of contexts and levels of complexity.

11.5. Challenges and Considerations

With great potential come formidable challenges. VR in social work raises several ethical, practical, and accessibility issues. Questions around data security, safeguards to protect vulnerable individuals, potential misuse, and ensuring equal access are all areas that need attention as VR continues to pervade the realm of social work.

Other challenges could include becoming overly reliant on VR and missing out on human contact, or the risk of further isolating individuals who cannot separate themselves from the virtual world—a concern already raised around technology addiction.

11.6. Shaping the Future of Social Work

Despite these challenges, the promise held by VR in transforming social work is undeniable. With proper and thoughtful application, VR can deepen empathy, expand therapeutic approaches, revolutionize education, and foster community understanding.

As we venture further into the new frontiers of social work, embracing disruption and harnessing the power of new tools like VR will be critical. Much like any transformative adoption of technology, it won't be without its risks and challenges, but the rewards could be monumental.

In conclusion, VR offers an entirely new dimension, a 'reality' that can be shaped, reshaped, and used to effectuate change—in the way we empathize, understand, utilize therapeutic interventions, train, and build communities. As the future of social work unfolds, undeniably, VR will play a significant role, guiding us through its next frontier.

Thus, it is imperative that we, as practitioners, researchers, educators, and policymakers, keep ourselves abreast with this rapidly evolving technology, breaking traditional boundaries, and deploying these advancements for the betterment of social work, thereby making a profound difference in the lives of individuals and communities we serve. The future of social work is upon us, and that future is virtually reality.

www.ingramcontent.com/pod-product-compliance
Lightning Source LLC
LaVergne TN
LVHW051632050326
832903LV00033B/4727